Feast yourself
SLIM

D0486664

Feast Yourself Slim may sound like a contradiction in terms, but you have only to leaf through the pages of this book to discover a wealth of recipes that will add zest to any healthy eating plan.

A meal consisting of Trout Timbale with Guacamole, Chicken Scallopini with Raspberry Coulis and Champagne Zabaglione with Oranges seems to have little in common with a slimming regime, yet the substitution of low fat alternatives for ingredients like butter, cream and cheese, judicious use of herbs, spices and other flavourings and sensible cooking methods means that that old enemy of the most dedicated dieter – boredom – can be banished forever.

Follow the advice in the recipes and cut off all visible fat from the meat before cooking, and use a nonstick pan without additional fat where possible. Where recipes specify skimmed stock, this is stock from which surface fat has been removed. The easiest way to do this is to chill the stock so that the fat solidifies and can be lifted off.

Colourful salads, some as main courses, others in supporting roles, are included, as are vegetables and vegetarian bakes. The collection concludes with a chapter of delectable desserts which are bound to be enjoyed by all the family. Approximate calorie counts are included with every recipe, proving that it really is possible to feast yourself slim!

CONTENTS

SOUPS FOR SLIMMERS	2
KEEP FIT WITH FISH	8
TEMPT WITH CHICKEN	16
FEAST ON VEGETABLES	24
SIDE SALADS	32
LEAN MEATY MEALS	36
LIGHT AND LOW DESSERTS	42

SOUPS FOR SLIMMERS

Here's a delicious selection of summer and winter soups that are high in flavour and low in calories.

Minestrone with Pesto

628 kilojoules/150 calories per serving

15g (¹/₂oz) butter

¹/₂ onion, chopped

1 leek, sliced

1 carrot, sliced

1 celery stalk, sliced

1 clove garlic, crushed

2 tomatoes, chopped

4 cabbage leaves, chopped

125g (4oz) green beans, sliced

1.5 litres (2¹/₂pt) chicken stock

30g (1oz) grated Pecorino or Parmesan cheese

Pesto

125g (4oz) fresh basil leaves

6 large cloves garlic, crushed

1 tblspn olive oil

1 To make pesto: Place basil leaves, garlic cloves and oil in a blender and process until mixture is very finely chopped. Pour mixture into an ice cube tray and freeze until ready to use.

2 Make the minestrone: Melt the butter in a large frying pan over moderate heat. Add the onion, leek, carrot, celery, garlic, tomatoes, cabbage and beans, cook for 2 minutes stirring constantly. Add the stock and bring to the boil. Lower the heat and simmer, uncovered, for 20 minutes.

3 Serve soup in large heated soup bowls, place a pesto cube in each bowl and sprinkle with the cheese.
Serves 6

Borscht

502 kilojoules/120 calories per serving

1 potato, peeled and cut into 1cm (¹/₂in) cubes

8 beetroot, peeled and cut into 1cm (¹/₂in) cubes

2.5 litres (4pt) chicken stock

30g (1oz) unsalted butter

2 onions, finely chopped

2 carrots, cut into 5mm (¹/₄in)cubes

250g (8oz) finely chopped white cabbage

2 large tomatoes, peeled, seeded and finely chopped

125ml (4fl oz) natural low fat yogurt

2 tblspn chopped fresh dill

1 Simmer potatoes and beetroot in chicken stock for 10-12 minutes, or until tender. Strain, reserving both stock and vegetables.

2 Melt butter in a saucepan, add onion, sauté until translucent. Add carrots, cabbage, tomatoes and reserved stock. Simmer, covered, for 20 minutes. Add potatoes and beetroot and cook until heated through.

3 Serve hot in heated individual bowls, with 1 tablespoon yogurt and a sprinkling of fresh dill in each bowl.
Serves 8

Minestrone with Pesto

Cauliflower and Coriander Soup

183 kilojoules/45 calories per serving

15g (1/2oz) low fat margarine

1 onion, finely chopped

250g (8oz) cauliflower, broken into small florets

1 tblspn chopped fresh coriander

2 bay leaves

l litre (1³/4pt) skimmed chicken stock

125ml (4fl oz) skimmed milk

1/4 tspn crushed black peppercorns

coriander sprigs for garnish

1 Melt the margarine in a large saucepan over moderate heat. Add the onion and cook for 2 minutes, stir in the cauliflower, coriander and bay leaves, cook for a further 5 minutes, stirring constantly.

2 Add the stock, milk and pepper and bring to the boil. Reduce heat and simmer uncovered for 20 minutes.

3 Cool mixture slightly, remove bay leaves and purée in a food processor or blender until smooth. Reheat soup and garnish with coriander.
Serves 4

Gazpacho

357 kilojoules/85 calories per serving

1/2 onion, roughly chopped

1/2 cucumber, peeled and seeded

1/2 green pepper, roughly chopped

1 clove garlic, crushed

1 tblspn chopped fresh coriander

440g (14oz) chopped canned tomatoes

4 tblspn tomato purée

200ml (7fl oz) tomato juice

1 tblspn red wine vinegar

1 tspn lemon juice

1/4 tspn Tabasco sauce

1 stick celery, chopped, for garnish

1 Place all ingredients, except celery, in a blender or food processor and blend for 30 seconds.

2 Chill soup before serving and garnish with chopped celery.
Serves 4

Vegetable Soup

84 kilojoules/20 calories per serving

2 litres (3¹/2pt) Vegetable Stock, page 6

100g (3¹/2oz) carrots, thinly sliced

100g (3¹/2oz) French beans, finely chopped

60g (2oz) cauliflower, broken into small florets

60g (2oz) peas

60g (2oz) broccoli, broken into small florets

salt

freshly ground black pepper

parsley for garnish

1 Bring stock to the boil. Add carrots, beans, cauliflower and peas. Simmer 5 minutes.

2 Add broccoli and cook 2-3 minutes or until tender.

3 Season to taste. Serve garnished with parsley.
Serves 4

Scallop, Tomato and Fennel Soup

502 kilojoules/120 calories per serving

4 tblspn olive oil

2 large onions, thinly sliced

3 small fennel bulbs, thinly sliced, reserve feathery leaves for garnish

3 cloves garlic, thinly sliced

1kg (2lb) ripe tomatoes, peeled and chopped

large pinch cayenne pepper

salt

2 litres (3¹/2pt) Fish Stock, page 6

8-10 scallops, sliced

1 Heat oil in a saucepan, add onion, fennel and garlic. Cook over low heat for 10 minutes, stirring occasionally.

2 Stir in tomatoes and cayenne, season to taste with salt. Add fish stock and bring to the boil. Reduce heat and simmer for 30 minutes or until fennel is tender.

3 Allow to cool slightly, purée in a food processor or blender and return to saucepan. Bring to simmer, add scallops and cook for 3 minutes. Serve hot, garnished with fennel leaves.
Serves 6

Vichyssoise

293 kilojoules/70 calories per serving

7g (1/4oz) low fat margarine

3 leeks, sliced

1 onion, sliced

2 large potatoes, peeled and chopped

1 litre (1³/4pt) skimmed chicken stock

125ml (4fl oz) skimmed milk

1 tblspn snipped fresh chives for garnish

1 Melt the margarine in a large saucepan over moderate heat. Add the leeks, onion and potatoes and cook, stirring, for 3 minutes.

2 Add stock, bring to the boil, reduce heat, cover and simmer, for 30 minutes.

3 Place stock mixture and milk in a food processor or blender and process until smooth. Chill and serve garnished with chives.
Serves 4

Curried Carrot and Chive Soup

293 kilojoules/70 calories per serving

15g (1/2oz) butter

2 large onions, chopped

8 carrots, chopped

6 parsley stalks, chopped

1 clove garlic, sliced

3 tblspn curry powder (more if desired)

2.5 litres (4pt) skimmed chicken stock

freshly ground black pepper

1 bunch chives, chopped

1 Melt butter in a large heavy-based saucepan. Add onions, carrots, parsley stalks and garlic. Sweat over low heat for 4-5 minutes.

2 Stir in curry powder and cook, stirring constantly, for 2-3 minutes.

3 Add stock, bring to the boil. Reduce heat and simmer for 30 minutes. Purée in a food processor or blender.

4 Return soup to saucepan, season to taste, reheat. Serve hot, sprinkled with snipped chives.

Serves 8

Cheese and Parsnip Soup

712 kilojoules/170 calories per serving

7g (1/4oz) unsalted butter

2 large onions, chopped

2 tspn caraway seeds

185g (6oz) fennel, chopped

1 large potato, scrubbed and chopped

2 sticks celery, chopped

500g (1lb) parsnips, sliced

1.5 litres (2 1/2pt) Vegetable Stock, page 6

60g (2oz) low fat Cheddar cheese, grated

salt

freshly ground black pepper

caraway seeds for garnish

1 Heat butter in a heavy saucepan, add onions and caraway seeds, cook until onion is soft and golden. Add fennel, potato, celery and parsnips, sweat vegetables for 3-4 minutes.

2 Add stock to vegetables. Bring to the boil, reduce heat, cover and simmer for 20-25 minutes. Cool, purée in a food processor or blender until smooth.

3 Return mixture to saucepan, bring to the boil. Add cheese, season to taste. Simmer until cheese melts. Serve hot, garnished with caraway seeds.

Serves 8

Cauliflower and Coriander Soup, Gazpacho

Chilled Indian Cucumber Soup

398 kilojoules/95 calories per serving

1 bunch fresh coriander

2 onions, roughly chopped

4 cucumbers, peeled, seeded and sliced

600ml (1pt) natural low fat yogurt

1 tspn curry powder

4 drops Tabasco sauce

salt

freshly ground black pepper

500ml (16fl oz) skimmed chicken stock

75ml (2 1/2fl oz) natural low fat yogurt and coriander leaves for garnish

1 Wash coriander thoroughly. Chop leaves and stalks in a food processor. Add onions and cucumbers, process until finely chopped.

2 In a large bowl combine yogurt with curry powder and Tabasco, season to taste with salt and freshly ground pepper.

3 Whisk chicken stock and cucumber mixture into yogurt. Cover and refrigerate for at least 2 hours.

4 Serve in chilled bowls and garnish with a dollop of yogurt and fresh coriander leaves.

Serves 8

Vegetable Stock

negligible kilojoules/calories

2.5 litres (4pt) water

3 onions, roughly chopped

4 sticks celery, chopped

4 carrots, sliced

2 courgettes, sliced

4 tomatoes, seeded and chopped

1 bouquet garni

8 black peppercorns

Place all ingredients in a saucepan. Bring to the boil, then simmer uncovered for 10 minutes. Strain and cool.
Makes about 2.5 litres (4pt)

Fish Stock

21 kilojoules/5 calories per serving

500g (1lb) fish bones from white fleshed fish

1 onion, sliced

1 stick celery, sliced

6 parsley stalks

60g (2oz) mushrooms, chopped

500ml (16fl oz) white wine

3 litres (5pt) water

Place all ingredients in a saucepan, bring to the boil. Simmer, uncovered, for 25 minutes. Strain. Cool, cover and refrigerate to allow any fat to rise to surface. Remove fat.
Makes about 3.5 litres (5pt)

Iced Watercress and Lemon Soup

167 kilojoules/40 calories per serving

2 bunches watercress, washed

1 onion, finely chopped

500ml (16fl oz) skimmed chicken stock

250ml (8fl oz) skimmed milk

2 tspn grated lemon rind

1/4 tspn freshly ground black pepper

125ml (4fl oz) natural low fat yogurt

1 Remove leaves from water and chop. Place in a large saucepan with the onion, stock, milk, lemon rind and pepper.

2 Simmer gently for 25 minutes, then purée mixture in a food processor or blender until smooth.

3 Stir in the yogurt and chill. Serve garnished with watercress sprigs.
Serves 6

Mushroom and Barley Soup

335 kilojoules/80 calories per serving

500g (1lb) fresh button mushrooms, sliced

1 small tomato, quartered

2 carrots, chopped

1 onion, chopped

2 sticks celery, chopped

1/2 tspn salt

4 parsley sprigs, chopped

90g (3oz) pearl barley

1.5 litres (2¹/₂pt) water

chopped fresh parsley for garnish

1 In a large saucepan combine mushrooms, tomato, carrots, onion, celery, salt, parsley sprigs, barley and water.

2 Bring to the boil, reduce heat and simmer covered for 1 hour. Serve hot and garnish with fresh parsley.
Serves 4

Spinach Soup with Garlic

711 kilojoules/170 calories per serving

5 cloves garlic, crushed

6 rashers bacon, chopped

1.2 litres (2pt) skimmed chicken stock

500g (1lb) cooked spinach

125ml (4fl oz) soured cream

1/2 tspn nutmeg

1 Place garlic and bacon in a large saucepan, cook over low heat 5 minutes.

2 Add stock, bring to the boil, reduce heat and simmer for 10 minutes; add spinach, simmer for a further 10 minutes.

3 Process mixture until smooth, add soured cream and nutmeg. Serve immediately.
Serves 6

Spring Onion Soup

879 kilojoules/210 calories per serving

8 bunches spring onions

125g (4oz) unsalted butter

1 eating apple, peeled and chopped

2 large cloves garlic, coarsely chopped

1.5 litres (2¹/₂pt) skimmed chicken stock

salt

freshly ground black pepper

125ml (4fl oz) soured cream

1 Coarsely chop 6 bunches of spring onions, reserve 2 bunches. Melt butter in a saucepan, add spring onions, apple and garlic. Stir-fry until soft.

2 Add chicken stock, bring to the boil. Reduce heat, simmer uncovered for 30 minutes.

3 Pour soup into a food processor and purée. Sieve back into the saucepan. Season to taste.

4 Slice remaining spring onions into thin rings. Add to soup, reserving a few onions for garnish.

5 Bring soup to the boil. Serve with a dollop of soured cream and garnish with reserved spring onions.
Serves 6

Tomato Thyme Soup

532 kilojoules/125 calories per serving

45g (1¹/₂oz) butter

2 onions, sliced

2 tblspn finely chopped fresh thyme

1 leek (white part only), sliced

2 sticks celery, sliced

440g (14oz) chopped canned tomatoes

500ml (16fl oz) skimmed chicken stock

Iced Watercress and Lemon Soup, Mushroom and Barley Soup

75ml (2¹/₂fl oz) natural low fat yogurt

thyme sprigs for garnish

1 Melt the butter in a large saucepan over moderate heat, add the onions, thyme, leek and celery and cook for 2 minutes.

2 Add the tomatoes and their juice, and the stock, bring soup to the boil, reduce heat and simmer for 30 minutes. Blend or process soup until smooth.

3 Return to the saucepan and heat through without boiling. Stir in the yogurt and ladle soup into four soup dishes. Garnish with thyme sprigs if desired.
Serves 4

Chinese-style Bouillon

837 kilojoules/200 calories per serving

315g (10oz) lean, boneless beef

4 tblspn tamari, see Kitchen Tips

1 tblspn flour

salt

freshly ground black pepper

1 tblspn mustard seed oil, see Kitchen Tips

1.5 litres (2¹/₂pt) hot beef stock

3 small carrots, cut into thin strips

185g (6oz) canned bamboo shoots, rinsed, drained and cut into thin strips

12 button mushrooms, sliced

6-8 shiitake mushrooms, sliced

90g (3oz) beansprouts

45g (1¹/₂oz) transparent noodles, cut into short lengths

10 spinach leaves, finely chopped

250g (8oz) firm tofu, cut into thin strips

1 tblspn dry sherry

1 Cut beef into paper-thin strips. Marinate in combined tamari and flour, seasoned to taste with salt and freshly ground pepper, for 10 minutes.

2 Heat oil in a heavy pan, add beef strips with marinade, sauté until browned on all sides. Add heated stock, carrots and bamboo shoots. Simmer for 5 minutes.

3 Stir in mushrooms, sprouts and noodles, cook for 5 minutes. Add spinach and tofu, heat through. Add sherry, adjust seasoning. Serve hot.
Serves 6

Kitchen Tips
Tamari is like soy sauce, but more strongly flavoured. It is available in health food shops, although soy sauce may be used as a good alternative.
Mustard seed oil is a highly polyunsaturated oil, available at speciality food shops. If unavailable, substitute with 1 tspn sesame seed oil and 2 tspn vegetable oil.
If fresh shiitake mushrooms are not available, use dried mushrooms soaked in lukewarm water for 15 minutes, then drained and sliced; or simply increase quantity of button mushrooms.

KEEP FIT WITH FISH

Fish is a perfect choice for those watching their weight. Combined here with other mouthwatering ingredients, you will find a host of interesting recipe ideas such as Mackerel with Chilli, Lime and Coconut Sauce, or Monkfish and Spinach Salad with Mango.

King Prawns with Pernod

398 kilojoules/95 calories per serving

1 tblspn oil

500g (1lb) uncooked king prawns, peeled and deveined, tails intact

1 clove garlic, crushed

4 spring onions, finely chopped

2 tblspn finely snipped fresh chives

1/2 tspn crushed black peppercorns

2 tblspn Pernod

parsley sprig for garnish

1 In a large frying pan, heat the oil over moderate heat. Add the prawns, garlic, spring onions, chives, pepper and Pernod.

2 Cook until prawns are no longer translucent, about 2 minutes, tossing frequently. Serve garnished with parsley.
Serves 4

Plaice Mousse

712 kilojoules/170 calories per ramekin

500ml (16fl oz) skimmed chicken stock

1 tspn oil

750g (1½lb) plaice fillets, skinned

4 egg whites

pinch of cayenne pepper

1 tblspn brandy

125ml (4fl oz) iced water

125ml (4fl oz) dry vermouth

500g (1lb) mushrooms, stalks removed, thinly sliced

1 onion, chopped

1 bouquet garni

3 tspn arrowroot, dissolved in 1 tblspn cold water

green beans, cooked to serve

1 Preheat oven to 180°C (350°F, Gas 4). Boil chicken stock until reduced by half. Allow to cool, set aside in pan.

King Prawns with Pernod

Trout Timbale with Guacamole

2 Lightly oil 8 ramekins. Process fish, egg whites, cayenne and brandy in a food processor. With motor running, add water and vermouth, purée until smooth.

3 Spoon mixture into ramekins, place in bain marie with boiling water coming halfway up the sides. Cover, cook in oven for 12-15 minutes. Set aside to cool slightly.

4 Add mushrooms, onion and bouquet garni to stock. Cook for 5 minutes. Stir in arrowroot and simmer for a further 2 minutes. Remove bouquet garni.

5 Unmould mousses onto individual heated plates, and serve with mushroom sauce and beans.
Serves 4 as a main meal
Serves 8 as a starter

Trout Timbale with Guacamole

1235 kilojoules/295 calories per serving

4 x 125g (4oz) skinless rainbow trout fillets

1 small ripe avocado, peeled, stoned and chopped

1 tspn very finely chopped red chilli

1/2 onion, very finely chopped

2 tblspn lemon juice

1/4 tspn white pepper

avocado and lemon slices for garnish

1 Line 4 x 125ml (4fl oz) timbale tins, using 1 trout fillet for each.

2 In a bowl, combine avocado, chilli, onion, lemon juice and pepper. Mash with a fork until guacamole mixture is reasonably smooth.

3 Fill each timbale with guacamole and securely wrap each filled timbale completely in foil. Place timbales in a large saucepan and add warm water to come about halfway up the sides of the timbales.

4 Slowly bring the water to just below boiling point, reduce heat and simmer for 2 minutes. Remove timbales and set aside to cool for 2 minutes.

5 Remove foil and gently unmould timbales using a knife to ease each from the edges of its tin. Place timbales on serving plates and garnish each with fresh avocado and lemon slices. Add finely sliced vegetables, if liked.
Serves 4

Piquant Oysters

209 kilojoules/50 calories per serving

24 oysters on the half shell

2 spring onions, roughly chopped

125ml (4fl oz) red wine vinegar

1 Place 6 oysters on each of 4 plates.

2 Combine spring onions and red wine vinegar in a food processor, process until spring onions are very finely chopped.

3 Place about half a teaspoon of sauce on each oyster. Serve immediately.
Serves 4

Chilli Lime Marinated Scallops

1757 kilojoules/420 calories per serving

24 scallops, lightly poached

12 cooked king prawns, peeled, deveined and cut into 2cm ($^3/_4$in) lengths

60ml (2fl oz) freshly squeezed lemon juice

60ml (2fl oz) freshly squeezed lime juice

2 tspn chilli sauce

rind of 1 lime, cut into strips

2 tblspn chopped fresh dill

2 tblspn olive oil

dill sprigs for garnish

1 In a medium bowl, combine the scallops and prawns with the lemon juice, lime juice, chilli sauce, lime rind, dill and oil, mix well; cover and refrigerate for 2 hours, stirring occasionally.

2 Serve on small plates and garnish with fresh dill.
Serves 4

Smoked Trout and Mango Salad with Chilli Dressing

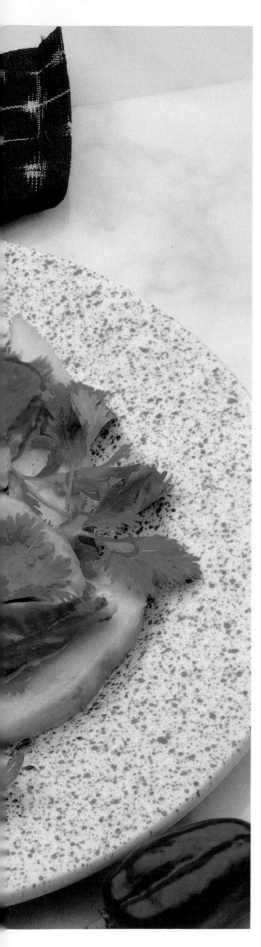

Smoked Trout and Mango Salad with Chilli Dressing

920 kilojoules/220 calories per serving

1 smoked trout, skin and head removed

2 medium ripe mangoes

1 small bunch coriander

Dressing

1 tblspn chilli sauce

1 tspn brown sugar

60ml (2fl oz) olive oil

2 tspn lemon juice

1 Pick out as many bones as possible from the trout, break flesh into small pieces. Peel mangoes, cut flesh from the stone and slice into thin strips.

2 Arrange the pieces of trout, strips of mango and coriander sprigs on a serving plate.

3 In a small bowl, mix together chilli sauce, sugar, oil and lemon juice. Pour dressing over salad and serve.
Serves 4

Prawn and Green Bean Salad with Dill Sauce

1316 kilojoules/315 calories per serving

1.5kg (3lb) uncooked prawns

125g (4oz) green beans, topped and tailed

2 sticks celery, thinly sliced

6 spring onions, sliced

3 tblspn chopped fresh parsley

lemon juice

4 hard-boiled eggs, roughly chopped

Dill Sauce

125ml (4fl oz) natural low fat yogurt

125ml (4fl oz) reduced fat mayonnaise

3 tblspn chopped fresh dill

freshly squeezed juice of ¹/₂ lemon

salt

1 Bring a large saucepan of salted water to the boil, add prawns, cook until prawns change colour, about 3 minutes. Drain and rinse under cold running water. Peel and devein prawns.

2 Plunge green beans in boiling water, allow water to return to boil, drain beans immediately. Refresh under cold running water, drain thoroughly.

3 Combine beans, celery, prawns, spring onions and parsley in a salad bowl, sprinkle with lemon juice, toss well to mix. Cover and refrigerate until ready to serve.

4 To make Dill Sauce: Combine yogurt, mayonnaise, dill and lemon juice in a small bowl, whisk vigorously until well blended. Season to taste with salt.

5 Serve salad cold or at room temperature with sauce in a separate bowl. Place chopped eggs in a small bowl and pass separately.
Serves 4

Kitchen Tip
When storing prawns, leave them in their shell. The shell acts as a natural insulator and helps retain moisture and flavour. Cooked prawns should be stored in the refrigerator in an airtight container or plastic food bag for no longer than 3 days. Uncooked prawns are best stored in water in an airtight container for up to 3 days. The water prevents oxidation.

Gravadlax

1506 kilojoules/360 calories per serving

500g (1lb) fresh salmon, boned

250ml (8fl oz) rosé wine

pared rind of 1 orange

pared rind of 1 lime

75ml (2¹/₂fl oz) walnut oil

2 tblspn chopped fresh coriander

1 tblspn crushed black peppercorns

4 tblspn chopped fresh dill

4 tblspn coarse sea salt

60g (2oz) brown sugar

1 Remove the skin from the salmon; lie the salmon flat in a dish. Combine the wine with the orange and lime rind and pour over the salmon. Cover and refrigerate for 1 day.

2 Remove salmon from marinade and pat dry with a paper towel. Brush oil over salmon and sprinkle with half the combined coriander, pepper, dill, salt and sugar.

3 Turn salmon over onto a large sheet of foil and sprinkle the other half of the herbs and sugar over salmon. Seal foil and refrigerate for a further 2 days before serving in thin slices.
Serves 4

Mussels with Vegetable Julienne

440 kilojoules/105 calories per serving

60g (2oz) carrots, cut into thin strips

60g (2oz) celery, cut into thin strips

3 tblspn chopped fresh parsley

4 cloves garlic, chopped

125ml (4fl oz) dry white wine

125ml (4fl oz) water

2kg (4lb) mussels, scrubbed, beards removed

2 spring onions, sliced into thin rings

salt

freshly ground black pepper

Gravadlax

1 Combine carrots, celery, parsley, garlic, wine and water in a large saucepan. Bring to the boil, reduce heat to a simmer, cook for 3 minutes.

2 Add mussels, increase heat to high. Cover, steam mussels, shaking the pan from side to side over the heat, until mussels have opened, about 5 minutes. Remove open mussels, cook remaining mussels a few minutes longer. Discard any mussels which have not opened after additional cooking.

3 Divide mussels between 4 heated deep bowls. Stir spring onions into broth, season to taste with salt and freshly ground pepper. Ladle over mussels, serve hot.
Serves 4

Kitchen Tips

To prepare mussels for cooking, scrub them under cold running water. Scrape off any barnacles, dirt or 'beards' with a sharp knife. Discard any cracked mussels or any that are open, even slightly, and which do not close tightly when tapped before cooking. Also throw away any mussels that remain closed once cooked.

Sole Seviche

691 kilojoules/165 calories per serving

500g (1lb) very fresh sole fillets, cut into 2.5cm (1in) strips

16 lettuce leaves

1 small Spanish onion, thinly sliced, rings separated

4 Divide lettuce between 4 serving plates, spoon seviche on top, scatter with onion rings. Serve cold.
Serves 4

Variation
This delicious Mediterranean fish dish 'cooks' in the citrus marinade. If preferred, replace the sole with other white fish fillets such as cod or plaice. The fish should be very fresh, and bought from a reputable supplier.

Bass with Vegetables and Cream Sauce

1130 kilojoules/270 calories per serving

7g (¼oz) unsalted butter, melted

1 bunch spring onions, cut into 2.5cm (1in) lengths

salt

freshly ground black pepper

4 sea bass fillets, 155g (5oz) each

juice of 1 lemon

4 medium tomatoes, chopped

60g (2oz) button mushrooms, chopped

4 tblspn chopped fresh parsley

155ml (5fl oz) dry white wine

125ml (4fl oz) reduced fat cream

1 Preheat oven to 180°C (350°F, Gas 4). Brush ovenproof dish, large enough to hold fillets in one layer, with melted butter. Arrange spring onions in the dish. Season with a little salt.

2 Season fillets with salt and freshly ground pepper to taste, sprinkle with lemon juice. Arrange fillets on top of spring onions, sprinkle with tomatoes, mushrooms and parsley.

3 Pour over wine, cover with foil, cook in oven for 20-30 minutes, or until fish is cooked through. Tip dish and pour liquid out of one corner into a saucepan. Keep fish warm.

4 Add cream to saucepan, bring to the boil, cook until sauce is slightly reduced and coats a spoon. Arrange fish fillets on heated plates, spoon over vegetables and pour over sauce. Serve immediately.
Serves 4

Mackerel with Chilli, Lime and Coconut Sauce

1924 kilojoules/460 calories per serving, without potatoes

8 x 155g (5oz) mackerel, cleaned and scaled

1 tblspn oil

2 cloves garlic, crushed

250ml (8fl oz) coconut milk

125ml (4fl oz) freshly squeezed lime juice

½ tspn crushed black peppercorns

1 tblspn chopped fresh coriander

1 tspn finely chopped fresh chilli

boiled baby potatoes to serve

1 To prepare mackerel: Cut off heads, make an incision from top to tail, being careful not to cut right through. Place fish cut side down and flatten out with palm of hand.

2 Heat oil in a large frying pan over moderate heat. Add garlic, cook for 1 minute. Add coconut milk, lime juice, pepper, coriander and chilli, bring to the boil, reduce heat, simmer for 2 minutes.

3 Add mackerel and poach for 3-4 minutes or until cooked through. Place fish on serving plates, pour pan juices over the top and serve with boiled baby potatoes.
Serves 4

Kitchen Tip
If unable to find coconut milk in your local supermarket, make your own: Soak 90g (3oz) desiccated coconut in 300ml (½pt) boiling water for 20 minutes, then press through a sieve. Alternatively, dissolve 60g (2oz) creamed coconut in 250ml (8fl oz) boiling water.

Marinade

juice of 8 limes

juice of 2 lemons

juice of 2 oranges

2 tblspn chopped fresh coriander

1 clove garlic, crushed

1 tspn chilli paste

30g (1oz) sugar

salt

freshly ground black pepper

1 Place sole strips in a dish large enough to hold fish in one layer.

2 Make marinade: Combine lime, lemon and orange juice, coriander, garlic, chilli paste and sugar in a bowl. Add salt and freshly ground pepper to taste. Stir well.

3 Pour marinade over fish, cover, refrigerate for at least 4 hours, or until fish is opaque.

Top: Monkfish and Spinach Salad with Mango
Bottom: Seafood Sausages with Tomato Sauce

5 In a large frying pan heat enough water to cover foil sausages. When simmering, add sausages and cook for 6 minutes. Remove with a slotted spoon, set aside.

6 Purée tomatoes in a food processor or blender. Heat tomatoes, tomato purée and Tabasco in a saucepan over moderate heat, until warmed through. Pour sauce on each serving plate top with sausages.
Serves 4

Monkfish and Spinach Salad with Mango

1047 kilojoules/250 calories per serving
2 tspn oil
3 tblspn soy sauce
1 tblspn honey
$^1/_4$ tspn crushed black peppercorns
60ml (2fl oz) red wine vinegar
4 x 155g (5oz) monkfish fillets, cut into 2cm ($^3/_4$in) cubes
1 red pepper, seeded and cut into strips
8 spinach leaves, torn into bite-size pieces
1 mango, stoned and peeled, cut into cubes

1 Heat oil in a large frying pan over moderate heat. Add soy sauce, honey, black pepper and red wine vinegar, cook for 1 minute.

2 Add fish pieces and cook for 3-5 minutes, or until cooked. Remove fish and set aside.

3 Add red pepper to frying pan and cook for 3 minutes, stirring occasionally.

4 Arrange spinach leaves, mango, red pepper and fish pieces in a serving bowl.
Serves 4

Seafood Sausages with Tomato Sauce

839 kilojoules/210 calories per serving
15g ($^1/_2$oz) low fat margarine
8 spinach leaves, leaves chopped
$^1/_4$ bunch watercress, leaves chopped
625g (1$^1/_4$lb) boneless fish fillets, skinned
1 egg white
3 tblspn skimmed milk
$^1/_4$ tspn ground nutmeg
1 tblspn chopped fresh chives
2 tblspn freshly squeezed lime juice
4 tomatoes, peeled, seeded and roughly chopped
2 tspn tomato purée
2 drops Tabasco sauce

1 Melt margarine in a frying pan over moderate heat, add spinach and watercress and toss for 1 minute. Transfer mixture to a bowl and chill.

2 Purée fish in a food processor or blender for 1 minute. Add egg white and process for 30 seconds. Add milk gradually while processor is running, then add spinach and watercress, process for 1 minute.

3 Place mousse mixture in a bowl, cover and chill. Remove cover and mix in nutmeg, chives and lime juice.

4 Cut 8 foil rectangles, about 25 x 13cm (10 x 5in) and lightly grease. Place teaspoons of mixture on each foil rectangle, roll up into a sausage shape.

Poached Salmon with Asparagus Topping

Poached Salmon with Asparagus Topping

1465 kilojoules/350 calories per serving

1 tblspn oil

2 cloves garlic, crushed

3 spring onions, sliced

340g (11oz) canned asparagus, drained and chopped

4 x 185g (6oz) salmon cutlets

1¹/₂ tblspn Dijon mustard

60g (2oz) mature Cheddar cheese, grated

1 Preheat oven to 180°C (350°F, Gas 4). Heat oil in a medium frying pan over moderate heat. Add garlic and spring onions, cook for 1 minute. Remove pan from heat and stir in asparagus, set aside.

2 Place salmon cutlets in a lightly greased baking dish and bake in oven for 15 minutes.

3 Spread top side of each cutlet with mustard, then spoon asparagus mixture on top. Sprinkle with cheese and return to the oven for 5-10 minutes or until cheese has melted.
Serves 4

Salmon with Garlic Sauce

984 kilojoules/235 calories per serving

2 tblspn olive oil

4 x 155g (5oz) salmon steaks

16 cloves garlic, finely chopped

1 red chilli, very thinly sliced

4 tblspn finely chopped fresh dill

salt

freshly ground black pepper

500ml (16fl oz) Fish Stock, page 6

dill sprigs for garnish

1 Preheat oven to 180°C (350°F, Gas 4). Heat oil in a frying pan large enough to hold fish in one layer. Add garlic, chilli and dill, sauté for 1 minute. Arrange fish on top, season to taste with salt and freshly ground pepper.

2 Add stock, bring to a simmer, basting fish from time to time. Cover, cook over very low heat until fish is tender, about 8 minutes.

3 Transfer fish to a heated serving dish with a slotted spoon. Remove skin, keep warm.

4 Boil pan juices over high heat until 125ml (4fl oz) liquid remains, about 10 minutes. Pour over fish, serve warm or at room temperature, garnished with dill sprigs.
Serves 4

15

TEMPT WITH CHICKEN

The chicken dishes in this section taste so good, it is hard to believe they are low in calories! Enjoy favourites like Chicken Curry with Yogurt, Rosemary Roasted Chicken with Carrots, or Normandy Chicken – all for under 375 calories per serving.

Baked Chicken Pieces with Orange Sauce

1403 kilojoules/335 calories per serving

15g (1/2oz) butter

3 chicken pieces, skin removed, broken into pieces

125ml (4fl oz) sweet white wine

125ml (4fl oz) freshly squeezed orange juice

1/2 orange, cut into thin slices

60ml (2fl oz) apple juice

2 tblspn freshly squeezed lime juice

1 tblspn honey

parsley sprig for garnish

1 Preheat oven to 180°C (350°F, Gas 4). Heat the butter in a large frying pan over moderate heat. Add the chicken pieces and cook for 4 minutes, stirring constantly.

2 Remove chicken, place in a baking dish and cook in oven for 20 minutes or until cooked through.

3 Meanwhile, add the wine, orange juice, orange slices, apple juice, lime juice and honey to frying pan. Bring liquid to the boil, reduce heat and simmer for 5-7 minutes or until sauce thickens slightly.

4 Remove chicken from oven and add to the frying pan. Turn chicken to cover in sauce, pour chicken and orange sauce into serving dish and garnish with parsley.

Serves 4

Chicken Medallions with Pimiento Sauce

921 kilojoules/220 calories per serving

4 chicken breast fillets

2 tblspn lemon juice

8 spinach leaves, stems removed

Sauce

125g (4oz) canned pimientos, drained and chopped

1 onion, chopped

2 tblspn tomato purée

1 tblspn natural yogurt

1 Preheat oven to 180°C (350°F, Gas 4). Brush chicken fillets with lemon juice and cut into 4 neat rectangles. Lay 2 spinach leaves on each fillet and roll up into a sausage shape. Wrap each roll in foil.

2 Bake chicken rolls in oven for 20-25 minutes.

3 Meanwhile, make the sauce: Purée the pimientos with the onion and tomato purée until smooth. Divide sauce into two bowls. Stir the yogurt into one bowl to make a pale pink sauce.

4 Carefully spoon equal amounts of each sauce on each plate.

5 Unwrap the chicken rolls and slice with a sharp knife. Arrange the chicken slices decoratively on top of the sauce.

Serves 4

Baked Chicken Pieces with Orange Sauce, Chicken Medallions with Pimiento Sauce

Chicken Curry with Yogurt

879 kilojoules/210 calories per serving

4 chicken breast fillets, skinned and halved

125ml (4fl oz) dry white wine

1 small leek, sliced

1 bay leaf

4 parsley sprigs

1 carrot, thickly sliced

500ml (16fl oz) water

2 tblspn sunflower oil

2 cloves garlic, finely chopped

2 tblspn grated fresh ginger

2 tblspn curry powder

3 tomatoes, peeled, chopped

1 fennel bulb, chopped

1 Granny Smith apple, cored, coarsely chopped

2 large courgettes, sliced

2 sticks celery, sliced

2 large carrots, sliced

2 large onions, chopped

250ml (8fl oz) natural low fat yogurt

salt

freshly ground black pepper

1 Combine chicken, wine, leek, bay leaf, parsley and carrot in a saucepan, add water. Bring to the boil, reduce heat to a simmer, cover, cook until chicken is tender.

2 Measure 375ml (12fl oz) of the liquid, reserve to make the curry, leave chicken to cool in remaining poaching liquid.

3 Heat oil in a flameproof casserole, add garlic and ginger, sauté until softened, about 2 minutes. Add curry powder, tomatoes, fennel, apple, courgettes, celery, carrots, onions and the reserved liquid.

4 Bring to the boil, reduce heat to a simmer, cook uncovered until sauce is thick, about 1 hour. Add a little more poaching liquid if sauce becomes too thick.

5 Remove chicken from poaching liquid, cut into bite-size pieces. Add to sauce, together with yogurt. Heat gently and season to taste.

Serves 6

Chicken Breast with Tricolour Vegetables

1089 kilojoules/260 calories per serving

1 tblspn olive oil

3 tblspn red wine vinegar

3 tblspn red wine

2 tblspn Worcestershire sauce

4 chicken breast fillets, skinned

4 courgettes, sliced

125g (4oz) yellow baby squash, cut into quarters, optional

1 red pepper, seeded, cut into small thin strips

1 tblspn chopped fresh dill

1/2 tspn crushed black peppercorns

1 tblspn honey

1 tblspn soy sauce

2 tspn tomato purée

dill sprigs for garnish

1 Heat the oil in a large frying pan over moderate heat. Add the red wine vinegar, wine and Worcestershire sauce, cook for 1 minute.

2 Add chicken breasts and vegetables and cook the chicken for 3 minutes each side. Add the dill and pepper, toss vegetables and remove them with a slotted spoon. Keep warm.

3 Add honey, soy sauce and tomato purée to the frying pan, increase the heat and cook for 2 minutes or until chicken is cooked through, turning chicken frequently to coat well.

4 Serve chicken with the pan sauce and place vegetables on side of plate. Garnish with dill sprigs.

Serves 4

Turkey Breasts with Citrus Sauce

1570 kilojoules/375 calories per serving

375ml (12fl oz) skimmed chicken stock

2 tspn chopped fresh rosemary

flour

salt

freshly ground black pepper

375g (12oz) turkey breast, cut into 12 slices

60ml (2fl oz) olive oil

1/2 small onion, thinly sliced

185ml (6fl oz) freshly squeezed grapefruit juice

125ml (4fl oz) freshly squeezed orange juice

1 tspn chopped fresh thyme

1/4 tspn chilli powder

1 Combine chicken stock and rosemary in a small saucepan. Bring to the boil, reduce heat to a simmer, cook for 5 minutes, set aside.

2 Season flour and use to dust turkey slices, shake to remove excess.

3 Heat 1 tablespoon of the olive oil in a frying pan, add 4 turkey slices, sauté until golden, about 4 minutes, turning once. Remove and repeat with remaining oil and turkey, cover, set aside.

4 Add onion to frying pan, reduce heat, sauté until softened, about 5 minutes. Add grapefruit and orange juice. Increase heat, bring to the boil, scraping up any browned bits from the bottom.

5 Strain chicken stock into the pan, discard rosemary. Add thyme and chilli powder, boil until liquid is reduced to 500ml (16fl oz).

6 Reduce heat, return turkey slices to the pan, cook until heated through, about 2 minutes. With a slotted spoon transfer turkey to a heated serving platter. Check seasoning of the sauce, pour over turkey. Serve immediately.

Serves 6

Turkey Breasts with Citrus Sauce

19

Rosemary Roasted Chicken with Carrots

900 kilojoules/215 calories per serving

4 x 110g (3¹/₂oz) chicken breast fillets, halved

salt

freshly ground black pepper

2 tspn chopped fresh rosemary

8 carrots, cut diagonally into 5cm (2in) lengths

15g (¹/₂oz) unsalted butter, cut into small cubes

2 tblspn skimmed chicken stock, warmed

rosemary sprigs for garnish

1 Preheat oven to 200°C (400°F, Gas 6). Rub chicken with salt and pepper to taste, sprinkle with rosemary, place in a baking dish.

2 Boil, steam or microwave carrots until just tender, arrange around chicken. Dot with butter. Drizzle chicken with stock, bake for 15 minutes or until cooked. Serve chicken garnished with rosemary.

Serves 4

Chicken Curry with Coriander Cucumber Balls

983 kilojoules/235 calories per serving

3 cucumbers, peeled

1 tblspn white vinegar

salt

2 tblspn chopped fresh coriander

2 tblspn olive oil

500g (1lb) chicken thighs, skinned

15g (¹/₂oz) margarine

1 onion, chopped

¹/2 red pepper, chopped

2 cloves garlic, crushed

2 tspn curry powder

1 Scoop out cucumber balls with a melon baller. Place in a bowl and sprinkle with vinegar. Season very lightly with salt. Add coriander, toss well. Cover, refrigerate until ready to eat.

2 Place oil in a frying pan, sauté thighs until cooked through. Remove from pan, set aside.

3 Melt margarine in frying pan, add onion, red pepper and garlic, sauté until vegetables are tender. Add curry powder, season to taste.

4 Return chicken to pan, sauté to heat and coat with sauce. Serve hot with chilled cucumber balls.

Serves 6

Chicken Breasts with Spring Onions

1214 kilojoules/290 calories per serving

4 x 155g (5oz) chicken breast fillets, skinned and halved

flour

45g (1¹/₂oz) unsalted butter

125g (4oz) spring onions, chopped

2 small cloves garlic, finely chopped

125ml (4fl oz) dry white wine

salt

freshly ground black pepper

1 tblspn freshly squeezed lemon juice

2 tspn grated lemon rind

1 tblspn chopped fresh parsley

2 tblspn fresh breadcrumbs

1 Preheat oven to 200°C (400°F, Gas 6). Place chicken breasts between layers of greaseproof paper, beat to an even thickness. Dust with flour, shake off excess.

2 Melt 30g (1oz) of the butter in a frying pan, add chicken, sauté until golden brown on both sides, turning once. Remove and set aside.

3 Reduce heat, add spring onions and garlic to pan, cook until softened. Add wine, bring to the boil, cook until reduced by half, scraping up any browned bits.

4 Pour half the sauce in a lightly greased baking dish. Add chicken, season to taste and sprinkle with lemon juice.

5 Spoon over remaining sauce, sprinkle with lemon rind, parsley and breadcrumbs. Dot with remaining butter. Bake for 15 minutes or until cooked.

Serves 4

Florence Baked Chicken

879 kilojoules/210 calories per serving

4 x 125g (4oz) chicken breast fillets, skinned

2 tblspn Dijon mustard

2 tblspn white wine vinegar

1 tblspn lemon juice

3 cloves garlic

1¹/2 tblspn chopped fresh rosemary

45g (1¹/₂oz) fresh breadcrumbs

rosemary sprigs for garnish

1 Preheat oven to 230°C (450°F, Gas 8). Place chicken in a shallow baking pan, bake for 15 minutes. Remove to another baking pan. Set aside. Reduce oven temperature to 140°C (275°F, Gas 1).

2 Pour 185ml (6fl oz) hot water into baking pan used to brown chicken, scrape up any browned bits. Pour into a measuring jug, remove surface fat. Reserve stock.

3 Place mustard, vinegar, lemon juice, 2 cloves of garlic and 1 tablespoon of rosemary in a food processor, blend until smooth. Add 2 tablespoons of reserved stock, blend briefly. Reserve remaining stock.

4 Pour blended mixture over chicken, bake for 40 minutes or until cooked, basting frequently.

5 Chop remaining garlic clove, combine with remaining rosemary and the breadcrumbs. Add 2 tablespoons of the reserved chicken stock. Mix well. Spread mixture on a baking sheet and bake until golden and crispy.

6 Serve chicken sprinkled with crispy crumbs and any juices. Garnish with rosemary sprigs.

Serves 4

Chicken Stew

1234 kilojoules/295 calories per serving

4 x 155g (5oz) chicken breast fillets, skinned and halved

1/2 onion, sliced

3 sticks celery, sliced

375ml (12fl oz) water

salt

freshly ground black pepper

440g (14oz) chopped canned tomatoes

185g (6oz) cooked red kidney beans

185g (6oz) cooked sweetcorn

1 Combine chicken, onion, celery and water in a saucepan. Add salt and pepper. Bring to the boil, then cover and simmer for 1 hour.

2 Remove from heat, cool and skim fat. Remove chicken, strain liquid. Wipe out pan.

3 Cut chicken into chunks, discarding any bones. Combine with strained liquid in pan. Add tomatoes, beans and corn, heat through. Serve hot.

Serves 4

Chicken Keema (Curried Minced Chicken)

1046 kilojoules/250 calories per serving, excluding rice

2 tblspn olive oil

1/2 green pepper, chopped

3 garlic cloves, crushed

375g (12oz) minced lean chicken

2 tblspn curry powder

large pinch chilli powder

salt

185g (6oz) sweetcorn

2 tblspn chopped fresh coriander leaves

Basmati rice, cooked, to serve

1 Heat oil in a frying pan, add green pepper and garlic, sauté over moderate heat until tender, about 10 minutes. Increase heat, add chicken, sauté until cooked through.

2 Mix in curry and chilli powder, season with salt. Cook for 2 minutes, add corn, cook until heated through. Sprinkle with coriander, and serve with rice.

Serves 4

Lemon Honey Chicken Kebabs with Yogurt Sauce

1256 kilojoules/300 calories per serving, excluding rice

15g (1/2oz) butter

2 tblspn honey

3 tblspn lemon juice

2 tspn apricot jam

2 tspn grated lemon rind

1/4 tspn crushed black peppercorns

4 chicken breast fillets, cut into 2cm (3/4in) cubes

2 red peppers, cut into 2cm (3/4in) pieces

saffron rice to serve

coriander sprigs for garnish

Sauce

125ml (4fl oz) low fat natural yogurt

1 tblspn freshly squeezed lemon juice

1 clove garlic, crushed

1/4 tspn ground coriander

1/4 tspn ground cumin

1 Melt the butter in a medium frying pan over moderate heat, add honey, lemon juice, apricot jam, lemon rind and black peppercorns.

2 Thread chicken pieces and red pepper cubes alternately on short skewers and place kebabs in frying pan. Cook for 1-2 minutes on all sides or until chicken is cooked.

3 To make the sauce: Combine yogurt with lemon juice, garlic, coriander and cumin.

4 Serve kebabs on a bed of saffron rice, pour sauce over and garnish with fresh coriander.

Serves 4

Lemon Honey Chicken Kebabs with Yogurt Sauce

Quail with Caper Dill Sauce

1361 kilojoules/325 calories per serving

15g (1/2oz) butter

1 onion, sliced

1 clove garlic, crushed

2 pimientos, cut into thin strips

1 tblspn honey

2 tblspn red wine vinegar

4 oven-ready quails, cut in half lengthwise

250ml (8fl oz) dry white wine

2 tspn Dijon mustard

1 tblspn chopped fresh dill

1/2 tspn crushed black peppercorns

10 capers

thyme sprigs for garnish

1 In a large frying pan, melt the butter over moderate heat. Add the onion, garlic and pimiento strips, cook for 2 minutes. Add the honey, wine vinegar and quails. Cook quails for 3 minutes each side.

2 Add wine, mustard, dill, black pepper and capers to the frying pan, cook until sauce thickens slightly and quails are cooked through.

3 Arrange 2 quail halves on each plate, spoon sauce over the top and garnish with fresh thyme.

Serves 4

Tarragon Chicken

837 kilojoules/200 calories per serving

2 whole chicken breasts, skin on, about 500g (1lb) each

1 large clove garlic, halved

1 lemon, halved

1 tspn dried chopped tarragon

salt

1 Preheat oven to 230°C (450°F, Gas 8). Rub chicken breasts with cut garlic and halved lemon. Gently loosen skin from breast, spread tarragon between flesh and skin.

2 Place chicken on a rack in a roasting dish, squeeze over some lemon juice, season to taste with salt.

3 Bake for 35 minutes or until chicken is tender. Stand at room temperature for 10 minutes.

4 Remove skin, slice meat off the bone in a single piece from each side of the breast. Serve hot.

Serves 4

Normandy Chicken

1250 kilojoules/300 calories per serving

1 tblspn vegetable oil

1 tblspn groundnut oil

4 x 125g (4oz) boneless chicken breast fillets, skinned and halved

salt

freshly ground black pepper

125ml (4fl oz) Calvados

3 tblspn cider vinegar

500g (1lb) dessert apples, not peeled, cored, cut into eighths

250ml (8fl oz) skimmed chicken stock

1 Preheat oven to 180°C (350°F, Gas 4). In a large frying pan heat both oils, add chicken, sauté over high heat until golden, about 8 minutes, turning once. Remove from pan, season to taste.

2 Pour fat from frying pan, add half the Calvados and all the vinegar. Bring to the boil, scraping up any browned bits from the bottom. Remove from the heat.

3 Place apples in a casserole, arrange chicken on top. Pour liquid in the frying pan over chicken, bake for 20 minutes or until chicken is cooked.

4 Remove chicken from casserole, keep warm. Pour apples and juices from pan into a food processor or blender, purée.

5 Pour into a saucepan, add stock and remaining Calvados. Bring to the boil, cook until sauce thickens, about 5 minutes. Divide sauce between 4 heated plates, arrange chicken on top.

Serves 4

Quail with Caper Dill Sauce

Chicken Scallopini with Raspberry Coulis

Kitchen Tip
Calvados is a French apple brandy. If not available, use ordinary brandy.

Chicken Scallopini with Raspberry Coulis

1214 kilojoules/290 calories per serving

4 x 155g (5oz) chicken breast fillets, skinned

2 eggs, lightly beaten

125g (4oz) dried breadcrumbs

185g (6oz) fresh raspberries

2 tspn raspberry jam

2 tblspn freshly squeezed lime juice

2 tblspn freshly squeezed orange juice

parsley sprig for garnish

1 Preheat oven to 180°C (350°F, Gas 4). Dip chicken fillets in the beaten egg, then dip the chicken in breadcrumbs, shake off any excess breadcrumbs. Bake coated chicken fillets in oven for 20 minutes or until cooked through.

2 Process raspberries, jam, lime juice and orange juice in a food processor until smooth.

3 Push puréed mixture through a sieve to remove the seeds, heat sauce in a small saucepan over low heat and serve with chicken fillets. Garnish with parsley.

Serves 4

Chicken in Red Wine

1193 kilojoules/285 calories per serving

750g (1½lb) boneless chicken breasts, skinned and halved

1 tblspn olive oil

1 tblspn honey

Marinade

375ml (12fl oz) dry red wine

1 tblspn olive oil

8 cloves garlic, crushed

2 tspn chopped fresh rosemary

salt

freshly ground black pepper

1 To make marinade: Combine wine, oil, garlic and rosemary in a large bowl, season to taste with salt and freshly ground pepper. Add chicken, cover, allow to stand at room temperature for at least 1 hour.

2 Remove chicken from marinade, pat dry with paper towels. Reserve marinade.

3 Heat oil in a nonstick frying pan, add chicken, cook until tender and golden on both sides, about 8 minutes, turning once. Place on a heated serving dish, keep warm.

4 Pour off any remaining fat from the pan, add marinade and honey, bring to the boil, scraping up any browned bits from the bottom. Cook until sauce thickens slightly.

5 Pour sauce over chicken, serve immediately.

Serves 4

FEAST ON VEGETABLES

Colourful, flavoursome and a valuable source of vitamins, vegetables can form the basis of a meal, as in the gratins and bakes in this section, or can be used as accompaniments. Explore their variety and versatility in the recipes for main course salads, and enjoy interesting flavour combinations such as Mangetout with Walnut Vinaigrette.

Potato and Leek Gratin

754 kilojoules/180 calories per serving

5 medium potatoes, peeled and sliced into thin rounds

250ml (8fl oz) chicken stock

2 large leeks, sliced (white part only)

2 cloves garlic, crushed

2 tspn finely chopped fresh rosemary

30g (1oz) low fat margarine

60g (2oz) dried breadcrumbs

1 Preheat oven to 180°C (350°F, Gas 4). Bring a large saucepan of water to the boil, add the potato slices and cook for 7 minutes. Remove with a slotted spoon and refresh under cold water, set aside.

2 In a small saucepan, combine the stock, leeks, garlic and rosemary. Bring to the boil, lower the heat and simmer for 3 minutes.

3 Arrange the potato slices in layers in an ovenproof dish and top with the leek mixture.

4 Melt the margarine and stir in the breadcrumbs. Sprinkle over the top of the leek mixture and bake in oven for 25-30 minutes.
Serves 4

Foil-baked Potatoes with Dill

670 kilojoules/160 calories per serving

4 medium potatoes, scrubbed, not peeled

60g (2oz) unsalted butter, melted

2 tblspn chopped fresh dill

salt

freshly ground black pepper

1 Preheat oven to 180°C (350°F, Gas 4). Cut potatoes into 2.5mm (1/8in) slices, but do not cut right through to the bottom.

2 Combine melted butter in a small bowl with dill, season with salt and freshly ground pepper.

3 Cut 4 pieces of foil, large enough to enfold potatoes comfortably. Brush foil with a little of the butter mixture in the centre.

4 Place a potato on top, spread the slices gently, brush with more butter mixture. Repeat with remaining potatoes.

5 Cook in oven until potatoes are tender, about 45 minutes. Open packages carefully to allow steam to escape. Serve hot.
Serves 4

Potato and Leek Gratin

24

Layered Aubergine and Artichoke Bake

Stir-fried Baby Squash and Spinach

272 kilojoules/65 calories per serving

8 spinach leaves, torn into bite-size pieces

1 tblspn oil

2 tblspn tarragon vinegar

375g (12oz) baby yellow squash, cut into quarters, or courgettes, sliced

1 Bring a medium saucepan of water to the boil. Add the spinach and cook for 1 minute, refresh under cold water, drain well and set aside.

2 Heat the oil and vinegar in a large frying pan. Add the squash and cook, stirring constantly, for 2 minutes.

3 Add spinach and cook for a further 1 minute. Serve vegetables immediately.

Serves 4

Layered Aubergine and Artichoke Bake

1382 kilojoules/330 calories per serving

2 aubergines, cut into thin slices

2 onions, sliced

375g (12oz) canned tomatoes

2 cloves garlic

2 tspn mixed herbs

315g (10oz) drained canned artichoke hearts, roughly chopped

2 tomatoes, sliced

100g (3¹/₂oz) cottage cheese

50g (1³/₄oz) ricotta cheese

60g (2oz) mature Cheddar cheese, grated

1 egg white

60ml (2fl oz) skimmed milk

parsley sprig for garnish

1 Preheat oven to 180°C (350°F, Gas 4). Place 125ml (4fl oz) water in a large frying pan over moderate heat. Add the aubergine slices and cook for 3 minutes. Remove with a slotted spoon and drain on kitchen towels. Pour away water, dry pan.

2 Return frying pan to heat, add onions, canned tomatoes, garlic and herbs, simmer for 5-7 minutes or until sauce thickens, stir in artichoke hearts.

3 Place half the tomato slices over the bottom of an ovenproof baking dish. Top with half the aubergine slices, then pour half the tomato mixture over the top. Repeat with remaining tomato slices, aubergine slices and tomato mixture.

4 In a food processor or blender, process the cottage cheese, ricotta cheese, Cheddar cheese, egg white and skimmed milk until smooth. Spread mixture over the top and bake in oven for 30 minutes.

Serves 4

Oriental Beef Stir Fry

1256 kilojoules/300 calories per serving

5 tspn oil

1 red pepper, cut into thin strips

1 green pepper, cut into thin strips

2 leeks, finely chopped

1 tblspn honey

2 tblspn soy sauce

625g (1¼lb) beef fillet, cut into strips

1 tspn sesame seeds

1 Heat 3 tspn oil in a large frying pan over moderate heat. Add the red and green peppers and the leeks and stir fry for 2 minutes. Remove with a slotted spoon and set aside.

2 Add the remaining oil, with the honey and soy sauce to the frying pan and heat.

3 Add the beef and stir fry for 3 minutes, or until cooked through.

4 Stir in sesame seeds and reserved vegetables, serve immediately.

Serves 4

Smoked Chicken and Watercress Salad with Croûtons

963 kilojoules/230 calories per serving

22g (³/₄oz) low fat margarine

2 cloves garlic, crushed

4 slices bread, crusts removed

185g (6oz) watercress sprigs

250g (8oz) smoked chicken, torn into bite-size pieces

2 tblspn low calorie French dressing

1 Melt the margarine in a small frying pan over low heat. Add the garlic and cook for 1 minute.

2 Cut each slice of bread into 9 squares and add to the frying pan. Cook on both sides until light golden brown, drain on paper towels.

3 Arrange the watercress and chicken pieces on a serving plate. Pour over French dressing and toss gently.

4 Arrange croûtons on top and serve immediately.

Serves 4

Kitchen Tips
There are numerous types of fats and spreads now available for the health conscious. When selecting a low fat spread for cooking, check the packaging to make sure it is suitable for heating.
Smoked turkey, which is sold in most delicatessens and the larger supermarkets, can be substituted for smoked chicken. Turkey is a very useful food for slimmers; weight for weight, turkey breast has less saturated fat than chicken breast, and fewer calories.

Oriental Beef Stir Fry, Smoked Chicken and Watercress Salad with Croûtons

Beef and Bean Salad

1758 kilojoules/420 calories per serving

315g (10oz) kidney beans, soaked overnight

2 onions, 1 chopped, 1 sliced

2 cloves garlic, finely chopped

2 tspn chopped fresh thyme

pinch cayenne pepper

1 bay leaf

1 tblspn olive oil

2 leeks, thinly sliced

750g (1½lb) fillet steak, trimmed of all fat and sliced into thin strips

250g (8oz) French beans, trimmed, cut in half

8 cherry tomatoes, halved

1 green pepper, cut into strips

1 lettuce

Dressing

185ml (6fl oz) red wine vinegar

juice of 1 lemon

2 tblspn Dijon mustard

2 tblspn honey

salt

freshly ground black pepper

2 cloves garlic, finely chopped

60ml (2fl oz) sunflower oil

60ml (2fl oz) olive oil

1 Drain beans, place in a large casserole with chopped onion, garlic, thyme, cayenne and bay leaf. Cover with cold water, bring to the boil. Boil vigorously for 10 minutes, then reduce heat to a simmer, cover casserole, cook for 1½ hours or until beans are just tender. Drain, rinse beans under cold running water. Set aside.

2 Heat oil in a nonstick frying pan, add leeks and cook for 2-3 minutes. Add beef strips and sauté for 2 minutes. Set aside.

3 Cook French beans in boiling salted water for 3-4 minutes. Drain and refresh under cold running water. Drain again.

4 To make dressing: Combine all ingredients, except the oils, in a food processor. Process for 15 seconds. Gradually add oils, process until well combined.

5 In a large bowl combine sliced onion, tomatoes, green pepper and beef. Add kidney beans and French beans, pour over half the salad dressing, toss well to coat. Make a bed of lettuce leaves on a large platter, arrange salad mixture on top. Serve immediately, with remaining dressing separately.
Serves 8-10

Tossed Mediterranean Salad

670 kilojoules/160 calories per serving

1 lettuce, preferably Lollo Rosso

10 stuffed green olives, halved

5 black olives, pitted and sliced

4 hard-boiled eggs, sliced

1 red pepper, cut into thin strips

2 sticks celery, cut into thin strips

Dressing

2 tblspn red wine vinegar

1 tspn honey

1 tblspn freshly squeezed lime juice

1 tspn olive oil

1 Wash lettuce and break into pieces. Arrange lettuce, green olives, black olives, sliced eggs, red pepper and celery strips on salad plate.

2 Mix together the wine vinegar, honey, lime juice and oil and pour over salad.
Serves 4

Tossed Mediterranean Salad

Salmon Toasties and Avocado

1633 kilojoules/390 calories per serving

2 x 210g (7oz) cans salmon, drained, bones removed

4 spring onions, chopped

2 tblspn chopped fresh parsley

1/2 red pepper, finely chopped

1/2 tspn crushed black peppercorns

1 tblspn lemon juice

8 slices bread, toasted, crusts removed

8 lettuce leaves

1 lime, sliced

1 avocado, peeled, stoned and sliced

parsley sprigs for garnish

1 Combine salmon, spring onions, parsley, red pepper, black pepper and lemon juice in a medium bowl.

2 Arrange salmon and toasts on a plate with lettuce, lime and avocado. Garnish with parsley.
Serves 4

Turkey Breast and Feta Salad

2072 kilojoules/495 calories per serving

1kg (2lb) cooked turkey breast, skin removed, cut into bite-size pieces

2 sticks celery, finely chopped

2 cucumbers, peeled, halved, seeded

12 large black olives, pitted, halved

250g (8oz) feta cheese, cubed

1 curly endive

1 small bunch watercress for garnish

Vinaigrette

3 cloves garlic, finely chopped

4 tblspn chopped fresh basil

1 tspn sugar

2 tblspn whole grain mustard

freshly ground black pepper to taste

60ml (2fl oz) lemon juice

60ml (2fl oz) red wine vinegar

60ml (2fl oz) sunflower oil

125ml (4fl oz) olive oil

Crab and Mackerel Salad with Avocado, Salmon Toasties and Avocado

1 To make vinaigrette: Combine all ingredients in a screwtop jar, shake until well blended.

2 Combine turkey, celery, cucumbers, olives and cheese in a bowl. Pour over dressing, toss well to coat.

3 Arrange endive leaves on individual plates. Spoon salad on top and garnish with watercress leaves. Serve immediately.
Serves 8

Crab and Mackerel Salad with Avocado

879 kilojoules/210 calories per serving

4 crabs, cooked

125ml (4fl oz) dry white wine

2 tblspn freshly squeezed lime juice

410g (13oz) mackerel fillets, skinned

2 spring onions, finely chopped

1/4 tspn crushed black peppercorns

2 tblspn lemon juice

1 medium avocado, peeled, stoned and cut into large pieces

1 tspn finely chopped fresh coriander

1/4 red pepper, chopped

orange or lemon rind for garnish, cut into thin strips

1 Remove the flesh from the crab shells and set aside.

2 In a large deep frying pan, heat the wine and lime juice over moderate heat until boiling. Reduce heat, simmer.

3 Add the mackerel fillets and cook for 4-5 minutes. Remove with a slotted spoon and set aside to cool.

4 Flake the fish and combine with the crab, spring onions, pepper, lemon juice and avocado.

5 Sprinkle coriander and red pepper over the top and garnish with orange or lemon rind.
Serves 4

Chicken Salad with Mango and Spanish Onion Dressing

775 kilojoules/185 calories per serving

500g (1lb) boneless chicken breasts, skin on

1 mango, peeled, stoned, flesh coarsely chopped

juice of 1/2 lemon

1 tblspn red wine vinegar

1 tblpsn olive oil

salt

freshly ground black pepper

radicchio lettuce leaves

1/2 small Spanish onion, chopped

1 Place chicken breasts under a preheated grill, cook for about 8 minutes, turning once, or until chicken is tender. Set aside to cool.

2 Combine mango flesh, lemon juice, vinegar and oil in a food processor. Purée until smooth, season to taste with salt and pepper.

3 Arrange radicchio leaves on a platter. When chicken is cool, remove all skin, cut flesh into strips. Arrange on radicchio leaves.

4 Stir onion into mango mixture, pour mixture over chicken. Cover and chill for 30 minutes.
Serves 6

SIDE SALADS

These crisp salads are perfect accompaniments to plain grilled meat or fish, or may be served solo with warm crusty bread for a delicious light, low calorie meal.

Tangy Cucumber and Coriander Salad

105 kilojoules/25 calories per serving

2 cucumbers, halved lengthwise, seeds removed

salt

4 tblspn coarsely chopped fresh coriander

Dressing

3 tblspn white wine vinegar

1 tspn caster sugar

1 tblpsn finely shredded lemon rind

salt

1 Slice cucumbers very thinly into half moons. Place in a colander, sprinkle with salt. Weight with a plate with a heavy object on top, such as some cans, stand 1 hour. Remove plate and weights, rinse cucumber, pat dry with paper towels. Place in a salad bowl.

2 To make dressing: Combine vinegar, sugar and lemon rind in a screwtop jar, season to taste with salt. Shake until well combined.

3 Add coriander to cucumber, toss salad with dressing to coat well. Cover, refrigerate for 2 hours.
Serves 4

Kitchen Tip
This salad actually improves in flavour when chilled, and can be kept refrigerated for up to 2 days. In this case do not add coriander until just before serving.

Mixed Salad with Anchovy Pepper Dressing

879 kilojoules/210 calories per serving

1 radicchio lettuce

1 round lettuce

60g (2oz) alfalfa sprouts

155g (5oz) feta cheese, crumbled

1 orange, cut into thin wedges

8 parsley sprigs

Dressing

1 tblspn olive oil

1 tspn crushed black peppercorns

2 tblspn freshly squeezed orange juice

3 anchovy fillets, mashed

1 Wash lettuce leaves and tear into pieces. Arrange the lettuce decoratively on a salad plate with the alfalfa sprouts, feta cheese, orange wedges and parsley.

2 Combine oil, pepper, orange juice and mashed anchovy fillets in a screwtop jar. Shake until well mixed, then pour over salad.
Serves 4

Mixed Salad with Anchovy Pepper Dressing

1 Arrange tomato slices alternately with basil leaves around the edge of each salad plate.

2 Place the onion rings in the centre of each salad and pour over combined garlic, olive oil, lime juice and pepper.
Serves 4

Mangetout with Walnut Vinaigrette

314 kilojoules/75 calories per serving

375g (12oz) mangetout, topped and tailed

4 spring onions, finely sliced

1/4 red pepper, finely chopped

1 clove garlic, crushed

1 tblspn walnut oil

1 tblspn tarragon vinegar

1 In a large bowl, combine the mangetout, spring onions, red pepper, garlic, walnut oil and vinegar.

2 Toss salad well and divide between four serving plates.
Serves 4

Fennel Salad

335 kilojoules/80 calories per serving

2 fennel bulbs

Dressing

2 tblspn olive oil

1 tblspn freshly squeezed lemon juice

2 tblspn finely chopped fresh parsley

1 tblspn finely snipped fresh chives

salt

freshly ground black pepper

1 Cut fennel bulbs into 5mm (1/4in) slices crosswise. Separate rings, place in a salad bowl.

2 To make dressing: Combine oil, lemon juice, parsley and chives in a screwtop jar, shake until well combined. Season to taste with salt and freshly ground pepper.

3 Pour dressing over fennel, toss to coat. Serve immediately.
Serves 4

Above: Mangetout with Walnut Vinaigrette. Right: Two Bean Salad with Light Cream Cheese and Lemon, Tomato Basil Salad.

Two Bean Salad with Light Cream Cheese and Lemon

628 kilojoules/150 calories per serving

125g (4oz) dried chickpeas

125g (4oz) dried pinto beans

2 tblspn finely chopped fresh parsley

1/4 red pepper, finely chopped

60ml (2fl oz) lemon juice

30g (1oz) low fat cream cheese

parsley sprig and lemon slices for garnish

1 In separate bowls, soak the chickpeas and pinto beans overnight in cold water. Drain beans and place in one large saucepan.

2 Cover beans with water and bring to the boil. Boil for 10 minutes, then simmer until cooked, about 1 1/4 hours.

3 Drain beans and pour into a large bowl, stir in the parsley, red pepper and lemon juice.

4 Transfer salad to a serving bowl and serve with the cream cheese. Garnish with parsley and lemon slices.
Serves 4

Tomato Basil Salad

335 kilojoules/80 calories per serving

2 large tomatoes, sliced and halved

30g (1oz) fresh basil leaves

1 red onion, sliced into rings

Dressing

2 cloves garlic, crushed

2 tspn olive oil

1 tblspn freshly squeezed lime juice

1/2 tspn crushed black peppercorns

LEAN MEATY MEALS

Meat can still be included in a low calorie diet as long as lean cuts are selected. Here you will find a wide range of succulent meat recipes to suit all tastes and occasions.

Green Peppercorn Steak with Mustard Sauce

1151 kilojoules/275 calories per serving

3 tblspn green peppercorns, drained

6 x 155g (5oz) beef steaks

Sauce

155ml (5fl oz) thick natural yogurt

1 tblspn hot English mustard

2 tblspn chopped fresh parsley

salt

1 Crush peppercorns with the blade of a knife, press onto both sides of the steaks.

2 To make the sauce: Combine yogurt, mustard and parsley in a bowl, stir until well mixed. Season to taste with salt. Cover, refrigerate.

3 Preheat grill, place steaks on a lightly oiled grill tray. Cook for 6 minutes, turning once, for medium rare.

4 Serve on heated plates with the mustard sauce.
Serves 6

Roasted Veal with Honey Glaze

1507 kilojoules/360 calories per serving

1.5kg (3lb) boneless loin of veal

2 tblspn apricot jam

1 tblspn honey

2 tblspn soy sauce

60ml (2fl oz) lemon juice

2 tblspn red wine vinegar

1 tspn crushed black peppercorns

1 Preheat oven to 180°C (350°F, Gas 4). Secure veal with string and place in a shallow baking dish.

2 Combine the jam, honey, soy sauce, lemon juice, red wine vinegar and black pepper in a small saucepan over low heat, stir until well combined.

3 Brush the veal with the glaze and bake in oven for 2-2$^1/_2$ hours, or until tender. Baste the veal with the glaze every 15 minutes.

4 Slice meat and serve with vegetables.
Serves 8

Kitchen Tips
The key to losing weight is not to cut all your favourite foods out of your diet, but to limit those that are fattening. For example, the occasional roast potato may be eaten provided it is cut into largish pieces to prevent too much fat being absorbed during roasting. Parboil, then roast the potatoes with 2-3 tblspn vegetable oil in a hot oven until cooked and golden. Drain well on paper towels before serving.

Roasted Veal with Honey Glaze

Bacon, Beans and Barley

1110 kilojoules/265 calories per serving

185g (6oz) pearl barley

1 tblspn oil

2 onions, chopped

6 lean bacon rashers, rind and fat removed, chopped

1/4 tspn cinnamon

1 tspn chopped fresh thyme

100g (3 1/2oz) button mushrooms, sliced

250g (8oz) canned red kidney beans, rinsed and drained

375g (12oz) chopped canned tomatoes

250g (8oz) tomato purée

1 tblspn chopped fresh parsley

1 Cook barley in boiling water until tender, about 30 minutes.

2 Heat the oil in a frying pan over moderate heat. Add the onions and bacon, cook for 4 minutes. Add the cinnamon, thyme and mushrooms, cook for a further 3 minutes.

3 Stir in the beans, tomatoes and tomato purée, cover and simmer for 30 minutes, stirring occasionally. Stir in the parsley and serve with the drained barley and Red Cabbage, below.

Serves 4

Red Cabbage

188 kilojoules/45 calories per serving

1/2 medium red cabbage

2 tblspn red wine vinegar

2 tspn caraway seeds

1/4 tspn nutmeg

6 chives, snipped

1 tblspn reduced fat double cream

1 tblspn natural low fat yogurt

chives for garnish

1 Place cabbage in a saucepan with 3cm (1 1/4in) of boiling water. Add the vinegar, caraway seeds and nutmeg. Cover and boil for 2-3 minutes. Drain well, toss with chives.

2 Serve with combined cream and yogurt and top with chives.
Serves 4

Lamb Rissoles with Cucumber Sauce

816 kilojoules/195 calories per serving

625g (1¹/4lb) lean lamb, visible fat removed, roughly chopped

2 slices bread, crusts removed, quartered

1 onion, roughly chopped

1 clove garlic, chopped

2 egg whites

1 tblspn chopped fresh mint

2 tspn white wine vinegar

salt

freshly ground white pepper

1 tblspn olive oil

Cucumber Sauce

1 cucumber, peeled, seeded, finely chopped

155ml (5fl oz) skimmed chicken stock

75ml (2¹/2fl oz) natural low fat yogurt

2 tspn cornflour

2 tblspn chopped fresh mint

salt

1 Process lamb, bread, onion, garlic, egg whites, mint and vinegar in a food processor until finely minced. Season.

2 Divide mixture into 12 balls, flatten into patties, cover and refrigerate for at least 1 hour.

3 Heat oil in a nonstick frying pan, cook rissoles for 6 minutes each side or until browned. Keep warm.

4 Add cucumber to frying pan, sauté for 1 minute. Add stock, bring to the boil, reduce heat, simmer for 3 minutes.

5 In a small bowl whisk yogurt and cornflour together, add 60ml (2fl oz) of the hot stock, then add to the frying pan, stir over gentle heat until heated.

Red Cabbage
Bacon, Beans and Barley

6 Add mint, season. Serve sauce separately with the hot rissoles.
Serves 6

Glazed Ham and Pork Loaf

1172 kilojoules/280 calories per serving

375g (12oz) lean ham

60g (2oz) dried apricots

500g (1lb) minced pork

3 tblspn chopped fresh parsley

125g (4oz) dried breadcrumbs

125ml (4fl oz) skimmed milk

Glaze

90g (3oz) brown sugar

3 tblspn apple cider vinegar

2 tblspn Dijon mustard

1 Preheat oven to 180°C (350°F, Gas 4). In a food processor or blender, process the ham and apricots until finely chopped.

2 Place pork in a large mixing bowl, add the ham and apricot mixture, parsley, breadcrumbs and skimmed milk, mix well.

3 Press mixture into a greased and lined loaf tin. Bake in oven for 15 minutes.

4 Meanwhile, mix together the sugar, vinegar, mustard and 60ml (2fl oz) water in a small saucepan over moderate heat. Bring to the boil, reduce heat and simmer for 10-15 minutes. Remove from heat.

5 Brush top of loaf with some of the glaze, return to oven for another 15 minutes, glaze again, repeat every 15 minutes until loaf has been in oven for 1 hour.

6 Turn loaf out onto a baking sheet, brush glaze over bottom and sides, cook for a further 15 minutes. Cool for 15 minutes before slicing.
Makes 10 slices

Variation
This meat loaf is equally delicious made with lean minced beef or chicken in place of the ham and pork.

Baked Lamb with Red Wine Sauce and Vegetables

Baked Lamb with Red Wine Sauce and Vegetables

1340 kilojoules/320 calories per serving

1kg (2lb) boned and rolled loin of lamb

2 tblspn redcurrant jelly

125ml (4fl oz) red wine

2 tspn finely chopped fresh rosemary

185g (6oz) yellow squash or courgettes, sliced

250g (8oz) green beans, topped and tailed

250g (8oz) broccoli, broken into florets

2 tblspn chopped fresh parsley

1 tblspn toasted pine nuts for garnish

1 Preheat oven to 180°C (350°F, Gas 4). Place the lamb in an ovenproof dish, bake for 15 minutes.

2 In a small saucepan, combine the redcurrant jelly with the red wine and rosemary over moderate heat and bring to the boil.

3 Pour half the red wine sauce mixture over the meat and return to the oven for a further 45 minutes, basting regularly with the pan juices.

4 Meanwhile, bring a large saucepan of water to the boil, add the squash or courgettes, beans and broccoli and cook for 1 minute. Remove vegetables with a slotted spoon and refresh under cold water. Arrange on a serving plate.

5 Remove lamb from oven when cooked, slice and arrange with the vegetables. Pour the pan juices into the saucepan with the remaining red wine sauce mixture. Bring to the boil, then simmer until sauce thickens slightly. Sprinkle parsley over lamb, pour sauce over and top with pine nuts.
Serves 4

Osso Bucco with Vegetables

1800 kilojoules/430 calories per serving

1 tblspn olive oil

1kg (2lb) veal shanks, sliced

185ml (6fl oz) dry white wine

1 onion, sliced

3 courgettes, sliced

2 carrots, sliced

2 sticks celery, sliced

2 cloves garlic, crushed

375ml (12fl oz) skimmed chicken stock

1 x 425g (13¹/₂oz) can tomato purée

1 Heat the oil in a very large, deep (preferably nonstick) frying pan, over moderate heat. Add the veal and brown on all sides. Stir in the wine and bring to the boil.

2 Add the onion, courgettes, carrot, celery, garlic, stock and tomato purée. Reduce heat and cook until liquid is reduced by half, stirring occasionally.

3 Add 125ml (4fl oz) water and continue to cook for 1 hour or until meat is tender. You may have to add extra water if sauce gets too thick.

Serves 4

Variation

This Italian veal stew also tastes good made with a knuckle of pork, although the calorie content will be higher. Skim excess fat from the stew and ask the butcher to slice the knuckle.
Traditionally the dish is sprinkled with a garnish of chopped fresh parsley, grated lemon rind and chopped garlic before serving.

Steak with Rosemary Cheese Butter

1089 kilojoules/260 calories per serving
45g (1¹/₂oz) low fat margarine
15g (¹/₂oz) butter
45g (1¹/₂oz) cream cheese
2 tspn finely chopped fresh rosemary
1 clove garlic, crushed
4 x 155g (5oz) beef steaks

1 Soften margarine, butter and cream cheese to room temperature. Beat until well combined, mix in rosemary and garlic. Spoon mixture onto a piece of foil and roll up into a sausage shape, freeze until ready to serve.

2 Grill steaks on a rack until just cooked. Slice frozen cheese and butter roll into four 5mm (1/4in) slices and place one slice on top of each steak.

Serves 4

Dilled Lamb Chops

1298 kilojoules/310 calories per serving
2 tblspn lemon juice
2 cloves garlic, finely chopped
2 tspn sunflower oil
2 tblspn finely chopped fresh dill
8 x 60g (2oz) lamb loin chops, all visible fat removed

1 Combine lemon juice, garlic, oil and dill in a dish just large enough to hold lamb chops in one layer. Place chops in the dish, turn chops several times to coat with marinade, cover, allow to stand at room temperature for 30-60 minutes.

2 Cook lamb chops under a preheated grill until done to your liking, basting with marinade from time to time. Serve hot.

Serves 4

Kitchen Tip

An increasing number of butchers and supermarkets now sell lean cuts of meat. All meat is marbled with fat, but take care to trim excess fat before cooking and use no additional fat when cooking by dry heat methods such as grilling or roasting.

Osso Bucco with Vegetables, Steak with Rosemary Cheese Butter

LIGHT AND LOW DESSERTS

Enjoy quick and easy delights like Berry Yogurt or Poached Fruit Compote or more extravagant ideas like Champagne Zabaglione with Oranges or Grand Marnier Soufflé for under 295 calories per serving.

Tangy Pear and Raspberry Cobbler

1235 kilojoules/295 calories per serving

4 pears, peeled and cored

1 tblspn lemon juice

250g (8oz) fresh raspberries

15g (1/2oz) low fat margarine

15g (1/2oz) brown sugar

60g (2oz) unsweetened toasted muesli

1 Preheat oven to 180°C (350°F, Gas 4). Sprinkle the pears with lemon juice and cut into 1cm (1/2in) pieces. Arrange raspberries and pieces of pear in four 125ml (4fl oz) ramekins.

2 Melt the margarine in a medium saucepan, add the sugar and muesli, mix well.

3 Spoon mixture on top of each ramekin, bake in oven for 15 minutes.
Serves 4

Honey Vanilla Ice Cream

963 kilojoules/230 calories per serving

5 egg yolks

2 tblspn honey

1 tspn vanilla essence

500ml (16fl oz) skimmed milk

8 halved strawberries to decorate

1 Mix the egg yolks with the honey and vanilla in a bowl set over saucepan of simmering water. Add the milk and whisk for about 8 minutes until mixture thickens slightly.

2 Pour mixture into ice cream maker and freeze according to instructions.

3 If no ice cream maker is available, freeze mixture in an ice tray for 1 hour, remove from freezer, beat mixture with electric mixer, return to freezer. Repeat this process every hour for three hours. Freeze until ready to serve. Decorate with strawberries.
Serves 4

Champagne Zabaglione with Oranges

712 kilojoules/170 calories per serving

2 large navel oranges, peeled and segmented

3 large egg yolks

30g (1oz) caster sugar

1/4 tspn cinnamon

125ml (4fl oz) champagne or dry sparkling wine

1 Drain the orange segments well.

2 Place the egg yolks, sugar and cinnamon in a bowl set over a saucepan of simmering water and whisk until mixture is pale yellow and slightly thickened.

3 Add half of the champagne and continue to whisk until foamy. Add the remaining champagne and beat for a further 5 minutes.

4 Divide the orange segments between 4 serving glasses, spoon the sauce over the oranges.
Serves 4

Champagne Zabaglione with Oranges

Tangy Pear and Raspberry Cobbler

Oriental Oranges with Yogurt

544 kilojoules/130 calories per serving

30g (1oz) caster sugar

60ml (2fl oz) freshly squeezed orange juice

1 tblspn freshly squeezed lime juice

2 tspn lime rind, cut into thin strips

2 tspn orange rind, cut into thin strips

8 canned pineapple rings in natural juice, drained and halved

2 oranges, peeled and segmented

125ml (4fl oz) low fat natural yogurt

4 small bunches of red grapes

mint sprigs to decorate

1 In a small saucepan, heat the sugar, orange juice and lime juice until simmering. Add the lime and orange rind, cook for 5 minutes, remove syrup from heat.

2 Arrange the pineapple and orange segments on each of 4 serving plates and pour a tablespoon of syrup over each serving of fruit.

3 Serve with yogurt and small bunch of grapes. Decorate with mint sprigs.
Serves 4

Orange Rice Cream

795 kilojoules/190 calories per serving

155g (5oz) short grain pudding rice

600ml (1pt) skimmed milk

1 tblspn finely grated orange rind

250ml (8fl oz) freshly squeezed orange juice

2 tspn honey

1/4 tspn ground cinnamon

125ml (4fl oz) skimmed milk, extra

8 sliced strawberries to decorate

1 Place the rice, milk, orange rind, orange juice, honey and cinnamon in a large saucepan. Bring mixture to the boil over moderate heat, stirring constantly. Reduce heat, cover and simmer for 40 minutes or until rice is cooked and the liquid is absorbed.

2 Stir in extra milk and cook until almost absorbed. Spoon into serving glasses and decorate with strawberries.
Serves 4

Grand Marnier Soufflé

1172 kilojoules/280 calories per serving

45g (1 1/2oz) butter

1 tblspn grated orange rind

60g (2oz) caster sugar

3 tspn cornflour

1 1/2 tblspn flour

1 tblspn freshly squeezed orange juice

3 tblspn Grand Marnier

375ml (12fl oz) skimmed milk

3 eggs, separated

3 tspn gelatine, dissolved in 2 tblspn warm water

fresh raspberries to decorate

1 Beat butter with rind and sugar in a small bowl until light and fluffy. Beat in the cornflour, flour, orange juice and Grand Marnier.

2 Heat the milk in a saucepan. Stir in spoonfuls of the butter mixture until mixture boils and thickens. Cool slightly, whisk in egg yolks and dissolved gelatine.

Left: Orange Rice Cream, Foamy Baked Apples.
Insert: Grand Marnier Soufflé.

3 Beat the egg whites in a large bowl until soft peaks form. Fold egg whites into custard mixture.

4 Lightly grease four 125ml (4fl oz) soufflé dishes and tie a band of greaseproof paper around the top of each, to stand 5cm (2in) above the rim.

5 Pour mixture into dishes, chill until set. Remove paper carefully and decorate with fresh raspberries.
Serves 4

Coffee Zabaglione

398 kilojoules/95 calories per serving

3 eggs, separated

75ml (2¹/₂fl oz) strong black coffee, cooled

60ml (2fl oz) Marsala

15g (¹/₂oz) caster sugar

1 Combine egg yolks, coffee and Marsala in a bowl, beat until smooth.

2 Beat egg whites with the sugar until stiff peaks form, fold into egg yolk mixture. Pour into 4 shallow champagne glasses, serve immediately.
Serves 4

Foamy Baked Apples

523 kilojoules/125 calories per serving

4 large green apples

60g (2oz) sultanas

1 large egg

125ml (4fl oz) freshly squeezed orange juice

orange slices and fresh raspberries to decorate

1 Preheat oven to 180°C (350°F, Gas 4). Wash and core apples. Using a knife, make an incision in the apple skin, cut right around the centre.

2 Place the apples in a baking dish, fill each centre cavity with sultanas and bake in oven for about 45 minutes.

3 Meanwhile, place the egg and orange juice in a bowl set over a saucepan of simmering water and whisk until mixture is slightly thickened and foamy.

4 Serve sauce with apples and decorate with orange slices and fresh raspberries.
Serves 4

Flambé Strawberries

377 kilojoules/90 calories per serving

15g (¹/₂oz) unsalted butter

1 tblspn honey

2 tspn Cointreau

¹/₂ tspn grated orange rind

2 tspn water

375g (12oz) strawberries, halved

2 tspn warmed brandy

1 In a frying pan, combine butter, honey, Cointreau, orange rind and water. Bring to the boil, add strawberries.

2 Sauté for 1 minute, sprinkle with brandy, light with a match. Baste strawberries with liquid until flames die down. Spoon into dessert dishes, serve immediately.
Serves 4

Apple Crumble

544 kilojoules/130 calories per serving

22g (³/₄oz) rolled oats, roughly chopped

60g (2oz) dark brown sugar

1 tblspn flour

salt

15g (¹/₂oz) unsalted butter, melted

625g (1¹/₄lb) Granny Smith apples

¹/₂ tspn cinnamon

nutmeg

1 Preheat oven to 200°C (400°F, Gas 6). In a small bowl, combine oats, 30g (1oz) of the sugar, flour, a pinch of salt and the butter. Mix well, set aside.

2 Peel and core apples, cut into 1cm (¹/₂in) thick slices. Mix in remaining sugar, cinnamon and nutmeg.

3 Place apples in a flan dish, sprinkle topping over. Bake in oven until top is crisp and golden, about 20 minutes. Serve hot.
Serves 6

Prune Soufflé

481 kilojoules/115 calories per serving

15g (¹/₂oz) unsalted butter, melted

60g (2oz) caster sugar

250g (8oz) pitted prunes

60ml (2fl oz) Armagnac or brandy

10cm (4in) strip orange rind

3 egg whites, at room temperature

salt

icing sugar for dusting

1 Preheat oven to 200°C (400°F, Gas 6). Brush a 2 litre (3¹/₂pt) soufflé dish with melted butter, sprinkle with sugar, rotate dish in your hands to spread sugar evenly. Set aside.

2 Combine prunes, Armagnac or brandy and orange rind in a saucepan with 125ml (4fl oz) water. Slowly bring to a simmer. Cover, remove from the heat. Allow to stand for 20 minutes.

3 Discard orange rind; blend prunes and liquid in a food processor to a lumpy consistency.

4 Beat egg whites with a pinch of salt until soft peaks form. Add 15g (¹/₂oz) sugar, beat until well incorporated, add remaining sugar. Beat until stiff peaks form.

5 Fold 2-3 tblspn of the whites into prunes to lighten purée. Fold prune mixture lightly but thoroughly into remaining egg whites. Spoon into dish and run your thumb along top inside to push mixture away from rim. This will enable the soufflé to rise more easily.

6 Bake in oven on a low shelf until golden and well risen, about 15 minutes. Dust lightly with icing sugar. Serve immediately.
Serves 6

Fresh Orange with Grand Marnier Snow

523 kilojoules/125 calories per serving

3 large oranges

4 egg whites

90g (3oz) icing sugar

60ml (2fl oz) Grand Marnier

1 tblspn freshly squeezed lemon juice

1 Grate the rind of one of the oranges, set aside. Peel all oranges, remove all pith and membranes. Work over a bowl to catch juices. Divide segments between 6 shallow champagne glasses, cover, refrigerate.

2 Beat egg whites with a hand-held electric beater until soft peaks form. Add sugar gradually, continue to beat until all sugar has been incorporated. Beat until stiff, then beat in Grand Marnier and lemon juice.

3 Place generous spoonfuls of the snow on top of oranges, sprinkle with zest. Serve .
Serves 6

Berry Yogurt

209 kilojoules/50 calories per serving

1 egg white

15g (¹/₂oz) caster sugar

250g (8oz) mixed fresh berries

125ml (4fl oz) natural low fat yogurt

mint sprigs to decorate

1 Beat the egg white with the sugar until light and fluffy.

2 Add the berries and beat until mixture is smooth, about 1 minute.

3 Fold in the yogurt and spoon into chilled serving glasses. Serve immediately, decorated with mint sprigs.
Serves 4

Poached Fruit Compote

712 kilojoules/170 calories per serving

500ml (16fl oz) fruity white wine

185g (6oz) seedless green grapes

185g (6oz) canned peach slices, drained

185g (6oz) strawberries, hulled and halved

15g (¹/₂oz) caster sugar

15g (¹/₂oz) butter, cut into pieces

1 tblspn orange rind, thinly sliced

1 Heat the wine in a medium saucepan over moderate heat until simmering.

2 Add the grapes, peach slices and strawberries and simmer for 30 seconds. Transfer fruit with a slotted spoon to a bowl and cover.

3 Add sugar to the liquid, boil over high heat until syrupy, about 7 minutes.

4 Swirl in butter pieces and orange rind and pour over the fruit. Serve immediately.
Serves 4

Index

Apple Crumble 46
Bacon, Beans and Barley 38
Baked Chicken Pieces with Orange Sauce 16
Baked Lamb with Red Wine Sauce and Vegetables 40
Bass with Vegetables and Cream Sauce 13
Beef and Bean Salad 28
Berry Yogurt 46
Borscht 2
Cauliflower and Coriander Soup 4
Champagne Zabaglione with Oranges 42
Cheese and Parsnip Soup 5
Chicken Breasts with Spring Onions 20
Chicken Breast with Tricolour Vegetables 19
Chicken Curry with Coriander Cucumber Balls 20
Chicken Curry with Yogurt 18
Chicken Keema (Curried Minced Chicken) 21
Chicken Medallions with Pimiento Sauce 16
Chicken in Red Wine 23
Chicken Salad with Mango and Spanish Onion Dressing 31
Chicken Scallopini with Raspberry Coulis 23
Chicken Stew 21
Chilli Lime Marinated Scallops 10
Chilled Indian Cucumber Soup 5
Chinese-style Bouillon 7
Coffee Zabaglione 45
Crab and Mackerel Salad with Avocado 31
Curried Carrot and Chive Soup 4
Dilled Lamb Chops 41

Fennel Salad 34
Fish Stock 6
Flambé Strawberries 45
Florence Baked Chicken 20
Foamy Baked Apples 45
Foil-baked Potatoes with Dill 24
Fresh Orange with Grand Marnier Snow 46
Gazpacho 4
Glazed Ham and Pork Loaf 39
Grand Marnier Soufflé 44
Gravadlax 12
Green Peppercorn Steak with Mustard Sauce 36
Honey Vanilla Ice Cream 42
Iced Watercress and Lemon Soup 6
King Prawns with Pernod 8
Lamb Rissoles with Cucumber Sauce 39
Layered Aubergine and Artichoke Bake 25
Lemon Honey Chicken Kebabs with Yogurt Sauce 21
Mackerel with Chilli, Lime and Coconut Sauce 13
Mangetout with Walnut Vinaigrette 34
Minestrone with Pesto 2
Mixed Salad with Anchovy Pepper Dressing 32
Monkfish and Spinach Salad with Mango 14
Mushroom and Barley Soup 6
Mussels with Vegetable Julienne 12
Normandy Chicken 22
Orange Rice Cream 44
Oriental Beef Stir Fry 27
Oriental Oranges with Yogurt 43
Osso Bucco with Vegetables 40
Piquant Oysters 10
Plaice Mousse 8
Poached Fruit Compote 46

Poached Salmon with Asparagus Topping 15
Potato and Leek Gratin 24
Prawn and Green Bean Salad with Dill Sauce 11
Prune Soufflé 46
Quail with Caper Dill Sauce 22
Red Cabbage 38
Roasted Veal with Honey Glaze 36
Rosemary Roasted Chicken with Carrots 20
Salmon Toasties and Avocado 30
Salmon with Garlic Sauce 15
Scallop, Tomato and Fennel Soup 4
Seafood Sausages with Tomato Sauce 14
Smoked Chicken and Watercress Salad with Croûtons 27
Smoked Trout and Mango Salad with Chilli Dressing 11
Sole Seviche 12
Spinach Soup with Garlic 6
Spring Onion soup 6
Steak with Rosemary Cheese Butter 41
Stir-fried Baby Squash and Spinach 25
Tangy Cucumber and Coriander Salad 32
Tangy Pear and Raspberry Cobbler 42
Tarragon Chicken 22
Tomato Basil Salad 34
Tomato Thyme Soup 6
Tossed Mediterranean Salad 28
Trout Timbale with Guacamole 9
Turkey Breasts with Citrus Sauce 19
Turkey Breast and Feta Salad 30
Two Bean Salad with Light Cream Cheese and Lemon 34
Vegetable Soup 4
Vegetable Stock 6
Vichyssoise 4

Editorial Coordination: Merehurst Limited
Cookery Editors: Jenni Fleetwood, Katie Swallow
Editorial Assistant: Sheridan Packer
Production Manager: Sheridan Carter
Layout and Finished Art: Stephen Joseph
Cover Photography: David Gill
Cover Design: Maggie Aldred

Published by J.B. Fairfax Press Pty Limited
80-82 McLachlan Avenue
Rushcutters Bay 2011
A.C.N. 003 738 430

Formated by J.B. Fairfax Press Pty Limited
Printed by Toppan Printing Co, Singapore

JBFP 252 A/UK
Includes Index
ISBN 1 86343 121 7
ISBN 1 86343 116 0 (Set)

DISTRIBUTION AND SALES ENQUIRIES
Australia: J.B. Fairfax Press Pty Limited
Ph: (02) 361 6366 Fax: (02) 360 6262
United Kingdom: J.B. Fairfax Press Limited
Ph (0933) 402330 Fax (02) 402234